THE END

HAMBURG 1943

HANS

ERICH

NOSSACK

THE END

HAMBURG

1943

TRANSLATION & FOREWORD
JOEL AGEE

PHOTOGRAPHS
ERICH ANDRES

A WINTERHOUSE BOOK

THE UNIVERSITY OF CHICAGO PRESS
CHICAGO AND LONDON

The University of Chicago Press, Chicago 60637
The University of Chicago Press, Ltd., London
© 2004 by The University of Chicago
Paperback edition 2006

Designed by Winterhouse Studio
Falls Village, Connecticut 06031

Printed in the United States of America
23   7 8 9
ISBN: 0-226-59556-0 (cloth)
ISBN-13: 978-0-226-59557-3 (paper)
ISBN-10: 0-226-59557-9 (paper)
Foreword © 2004 by Joel Agee.
Originally published in German as *Der Untergang: Hamburg 1943*
by Suhrkamp Verlag. © 1948 All rights reserved.

Denkmalschutzamt, Hamburg Bildarchiv. Photographs: Erich Andres.
The publication of this work was supported by a grant from the Goethe-Institut.
The translation of the lines from the *Odyssey* on page 11 is by Samuel Butler.

Library of Congress Cataloging-in-Publication Data
Nossack, Hans Erich, 1901–1977
   [Untergang. English]
   The end : Hamburg 1943 / Hans Erich Nossack ; translated by Joel Agee ;
photographs by Erich Andres ; foreword by Joel Agee.
     p. cm.
   "A Winterhouse book."
     ISBN 0-226-59556-0 (alk. paper)
     1. Nossack, Hans Erich, 1901–1977
  2. Hamburg (Germany)—History—Bombardment, 1940–1945—
Personal narratives, German.
   3. World War, 1939–1945—Destruction and pillage—Germany—Hamburg.
   4. Hamburg (Germany)—History—20th century. I. Title: Hamburg, 1943. II. Title.
   D757.9.H3N68 2005
   940.54′ 213515—dc22   2004005284

CONTENTS

In today's world, personal truth is the only reality.
To stand by that truth — to declare it — is revolutionary.

HANS ERICH NOSSACK

THE END

JOEL AGEE

FOREWORD

Half a century ago, when I was fifteen years old, I read a collection of "reports"—that is what they were called on the flyleaf—titled *Interview mit dem Tode,* "An Interview with Death," by an author named Hans Erich Nossack. I was living in Berlin then, surrounded by many ruins left over from World War Two. It may be that the knowledge of so much violent death in my neighborhood not long ago was in part what attracted me to that title, even before I discovered how much of the book had to do with the enigma those ruins represented to me.

The reports were unlike anything I would have associated with that word. All but one of them were works of fiction, some of it quite fantastical, and the single piece of reportage proper, titled *Der Untergang*[1] — an account of the destruction of Hamburg by Allied bombers in July 1943—gave way, intermittently, to passages written in the language of dreams and fairy tales. This refusal to limit the meaning of "report" to the transmission of facts was, for me, a revelation almost as startling as the narrator's voice, which was so personal, quiet, and tender, even when speaking about calamity. Although maybe that stillness was itself an aftereffect of disaster:

> Already during the night and at daybreak the first refugees had arrived.... They brought with them an uncanny silence. No one dared to question these figures seated by the edge of the road. Just wanting to offer them help seemed too loud an action.

I translated the essay on Hamburg when I was in my early thirties. I was living in New York then. I'm not sure why I took on this task. It was not with the intention of publishing the piece. Probably my motive was to share it with friends and my wife, for no other reason than that I liked it. But I can't help thinking that my returning to Nossack's book at that time, and my choosing to translate that part of it, had something to do with the war in Vietnam, or rather with the language in which that war was discussed: militant language for war and against it, rational language of numbers and quantities, analytical language, newspaper language, speechwriters' language. In that Babel of rhetorics, I must have remembered the windless calm in Nossack's account and opened his book to see how he had managed to speak of his ordeal without complaint and without accusation and yet with an authority that compels a reciprocal calm in the reader.

THE END

I did send the manuscript to some publishers a few years later. No one was interested. Previous translations of Nossack's novels, though respectfully reviewed, had reached very few readers, as does most foreign fiction in the United States—that was one reason. But aside from that, I was told, Americans just weren't prepared to sympathize with a German description of the suffering of Germans in World War Two.

Three decades later, in November 2002, Nossack's name was brought to the attention of American readers when *The New Yorker* published "Reflections: A Natural History of Destruction" by the highly regarded and widely read German novelist W. G. Sebald. The article, based on a series of lectures Sebald had given in Zurich titled "Air War and Literature," criticized postwar German literature for consigning to near-total oblivion the horrors inflicted by Allied bombers on the defenseless population of cities like Hamburg and Dresden. "The darkest aspects of the final act of destruction," Sebald wrote, "remained under a kind of taboo like a shameful family secret, a secret that perhaps could not even be privately acknowledged." For nearly four decades, he said, all public discussion of this enormous event was confined to the occasional delicate mention of "the catastrophe." No small part of the blame had to be laid at the doorstep of those whose vocation it should have been to keep the collective memory alive—the writers. There were a few—five, in Sebald's count—who did venture to break the taboo by writing about the bombs and the fires and the degradation of life in the ruins, but even here there was a tendency to gild the unbearable truth with metaphysical musings, Symbolist jargon, romantic grandiosity, or avant-gardist language games. Only two authors—Heinrich Böll and Hans Erich Nossack—met Sebald's criteria for a responsible literature in the face of total destruction, and it is Nossack's short masterpiece, in the main, that is held up in Sebald's essay as a worthy contribution to a "natural history of destruction."[2]

It is worth taking a closer look at Sebald's thesis because it espouses a program in which Nossack cannot be enlisted without misunderstanding him. "On the Natural History of Destruction" was the proposed title for a report Solly Zuckerman, a doctor of medicine and zoology who had advised the British government on aerial bombing, had intended to write after visiting the ruined city of Cologne. Apparently he was so overwhelmed by what he had seen that he was unable to deliver the article. "My first view of Cologne," he wrote decades later in his autobiography, "cried out for a more eloquent piece than I could ever have written."[3] Sebald does not speculate as to why the scientifically trained Zuckerman was unable to write an empirical report but proceeds to undertake the task himself: "How ought such a natural history of destruction to begin? With a summary of the technical, organizational, and political prerequisites for carrying out large-scale air raids? With a scientific account of the previously unknown phenomenon of the firestorms? With a pathographical record of typical

THE END

modes of death, or with behaviorist studies of the instincts of flight and homecoming?"[4]

I don't imagine this is the type of eloquence Solly Zuckerman lacked. More likely he found himself unable to write because what he had to say could not be expressed in dispassionate, "objective" terms. Is it not conceivable that in the necropolis that had once been Cologne, or more likely when he sat down to write his report in the less severely ruined city of London, the enormity of what he had witnessed rose up in him as an inchoate scream or lament, and that this urgency demanded that he speak from the fullness of the heart or not at all? I am guessing, of course. But that Nossack, three months after Hamburg was incinerated, found himself at just such a threshold is not a matter of conjecture:

> I feel that I have been given a mandate to render an account. Let no one ask me why I presume to speak of a mandate: I cannot answer that. I feel that my mouth would remain closed forever if I did not take care of this first.

This is not the voice of a neutral observer. It is the voice of a witness—not in the usual, juridical sense, but in the confessional sense of religious parlance, although he brings no good news and says nothing of God: one who stands surety, with his soul and his life if need be, for a truth that might otherwise not be believed.

Sebald praises Nossack for being, on the whole, "concerned with plain facts: the season of the year, the weather, ... the physical and mental condition of refugees from the cities, the burnt-out scenery, chimneys that curiously remain standing, washing put out to dry on a rack outside the kitchen window...."[5] Here, for comparison, is Nossack:

> Why are there no smells on the stairs any longer? Why is there no laundry drying on the rack outside the kitchen window?... Wasn't there in every one of these numberless apartments, whose contours were now discernible only in what was left of the walls, a housewife who polished the floors and dusted the furniture day in, day out; who was afraid of her neighbors yet wanted to be envied by them? And why are the chimneys still there, meaningless and without smoke? But there's no stove left. What did we cook for? And no beds either! Why did we sleep? Why did we sustain ourselves? Why did we collect provision and save money? Everything that men have to say about this is a lie. It is not permissible to talk about it except in the language of women.

These are not "plain facts." It is the little word "I" at the start of his record and the presence, throughout, of a vulnerable conscience intent on being true to itself that make all the difference between objective reporting and authentic witness. That facts are nevertheless accounted for by such a witness—

scrupulously—is self-evident. Why would he lie or embellish a truth that already exceeds the bounds of imagination? Those who did so in their writing—Sebald cites some egregious examples—were not close enough to the event to be chastened by its sheer horror.

But let me not discount the part that imagination plays in Nossack's chronicle. He uses it frequently and freely. There are passages that might be termed mystical or surreal because they depart from the plane of realistic description altogether. These are no less concerned with telling the truth than those that record concrete data and tangible facts. They are attempts at describing an experience for which no ready language exists, because it takes place on the other side of an abyss that divides those who have lost everything from those "who still have a past from which they derive their standard for tomorrow." What comes across to us is an uncanny message of liberation: "We have become present." It appears from Nossack's account that for a brief period many survivors experienced a state of consciousness in which class prejudice and the masks of convention, fear of authority and the very notion of an enemy had fallen away, leaving only the lineaments of an archetypal humanity:

> But the visage of man in those days—who would dare to forget it. The eyes had grown larger and transparent, as they appear in icons. The cold, meanly divisive window glass was shattered, and through the wide openings the infinite

behind man wafted unhindered into the endlessness before him and hallowed his countenance for the passage of what is beyond time. Let us cast this visage as a constellation into the sky, to remind us of our last chance before everything turns into a faceless mass.

There are other surprises in Nossack's narrative—the most estranging, perhaps, for a contemporary reader, being the absence of any mention of the Nazis or Germany's guilt in provoking the retribution it was now receiving. I can only guess at the reasons for this. Nossack's contempt for "the authorities," for the state altogether, is too explicitly stated to allow for the explanation that he was motivated by caution. More likely, three months after an event whose violence had made a shambles of every pretension, every noble or ignoble aspiration, indeed every concept of order, his perspective was radically apolitical.

Strange, too, perhaps especially for readers of our time who live in a world of replaceable and disposable goods, is the almost keening tone of long passages of lament over the loss of things, from the most ordinary items of household use to works of art and objects of fine handicraft that "shared their existence" with Nossack and his wife. After all, many people lost children or spouses or friends; what is the loss of even the most treasured object compared with that? But maybe this is not so hard to understand if one tries to imagine the totality of the loss.

THE END

"Nothing was left, not a single trinket of all the things that we loved and that belonged with us. If there had been such a little something, how we would have caressed it; it would have been imbued with the essence of all the other things." Nothing. This word has a terrible resonance if one conceives it to mean what it does here: the absence of everything familiar, everything we call our own. Everything.

The impeccable witness to the destruction of Hamburg was an unreliable source of information about his own life—or perhaps I should say, about his biography. For he made a distinction between the "statistical," merely factual biography, dependably registered at various government agencies, and the "true" biography—"as 'auto' as possible"—that was his life's work. The conventional biography was that of a coffee merchant and, later, a professional writer of considerable renown, a founding member of three academies and vice-president of a fourth, an active member of the PEN Club, decorated with the Pour le Merite Medal, the recipient of two of the most coveted literary prizes Germany had to offer—in short, a model citizen. The subject of the "inner" (auto-) biography was a loner who fished at night in the "exterritorial" waters of the imagination, always in search of his own truth—a poet. The poet told some fibs and half-truths about himself—a sterner judge would call them lies—in several letters, a speech, and occasional articles. The voluminous secondary literature that developed around him repeated these self-stylizations and amplified them into something of a myth, with Nossack's tacit compliance. One of that myth's ingredients was a legend according to which the Nazis imposed an edict denying him the right to publish. In fact, he applied to them for that right, and they granted it but then prevented him from publishing a volume of poems on the grounds that there was a shortage of paper. A second legend had it that everything he had written before the fall of Hamburg had been destroyed in the flames, while actually five plays and numerous poems were saved, probably with friends living outside of Hamburg. The motive for these mystifications is not easy to determine: he called himself "the best camouflaged writer in Germany." But for truth of the kind that mattered to Nossack—the personal truth of a conscience engaged in scrupulous self-reckoning—we must turn to his work, not his public persona. Nossack spoke of the bombing of Hamburg as a new beginning for him, both personal and artistic. How could it not have been that? Here we don't need to doubt his word. His earlier dramatic work was under the impress of Strindberg and the mystical expressionist Ernst Barlach, while the novels and stories he wrote afterward are haunted (cheerfully sometimes) by the lure of a fundamental homelessness and anonymity that are Nossack's point of departure in *Der Untergang.*

After his death in 1978, Nossack's austere, introverted fiction fell into disfavor with an affluent generation that had no

THE END

memory of the war and no interest in exploring the region Nossack called "the uninsurable." He might well have been forgotten entirely if Sebald had not championed him and if Germans did not have the laudable custom of commemorating artists and writers of note on the occasion of their hundredth birthday. In January 2001, the month of his centenary, many newspapers carried stories about him, with titles like "Neither Right nor Left" and "A Courageous and Sober Archeologist of Conscience." One writer mournfully identified him with a class of authors young readers discount as the kind "my grandmother used to read." That is of course an assessment that applies equally to Kafka, Musil, and Camus, writers with whom Nossack has been frequently compared. At least two of his early works put him particularly in Camus's company: the still untranslated novel *Spirale*[6] and that luminous first collection of stories, *Interview mit dem Tode,* of which *Der Untergang* is the penultimate chapter.

Nossack's conception of the writer's role was, if anything, bleaker than Camus's. It was that of a combatant in a guerilla war for the preservation of human interiority, a scout who reconnoiters the social landscape and sends out messages to other clandestine resisters. Yet there was in those messages a serenity and even, in his later work, a contentment that seemed to say, "This silence, this emptiness that people dread, it's an openness, one can live in it, it's not so bad." Not that he would say this outright: it would be too loud an assertion and could be misunderstood as mere counsel on how to get by. Still, something like that can be heard, here and there, in the eerie equanimity of the voice that speaks to us from the ruins of Hamburg. Its tone, especially in the concluding pages, bears no relation to what most of us know or can imagine of disaster. It is the voice of a man who has crossed the river Styx and returned from the land of the dead. He would not say this of himself outright either, but I believe it is true. Why else would the last "report" in his "Interview with Death" tell of Orpheus ascending from the Underworld? The poet's steps halt at the threshold of life, he turns around and sees ... "Eurydice," we are prompted to say, because that's how the story has always been told. But she whom he thinks to behold is Persephone, the queen of the dead, before whose throne he had sung and who had interceded for him with Hades, the king, to release the abducted Eurydice. Not that we are permitted to believe that the queen really followed him. But from now on he will sing of her beauty—under camouflage, to be sure. The living are not to be trusted.

THE END

1. The word is commonly translated as "destruction" or "downfall," but its meaning here encompasses total collective ruin, with apocalyptic implications. Hence my choice of *The End* for the English title.

2. After its publication in book form (*Luftkrieg und Literatur* [Carl Hanser Verlag, 1999]; English-language edition, *On the Natural History of Destruction* [Random House, 2003]), Sebald's thesis was widely discussed and occasionally contested in Germany, notably by Volker Hage, who demonstrated that substantially more writers than those cited by Sebald had written about the trauma of aerial bombardment. Volker Hage, *Hamburg 1943: Literarische Zeugnisse zum Feuersturm* (S. Fischer, 2003), and *Zeugen der Zerstörung: Die Literaten und der Luftkrieg*. Essays und Gespräche (S. Fischer, 2003).

3. Solly Zuckerman, quoted in Sebald, *Natural History of Destruction*, 31.

4. Sebald, *Natural History of Destruction*, 33. The questioning tone of these sentences suggests ambivalence, perhaps disapproval, of what they propose, but with the very next sentence Sebald goes on to praise Nossack for having described the movements of refugees in such a way that they could indeed serve as material for a behaviorist study. This would be unobjectionable if he did not also chide him, in passing, for not adhering consistently to this documentary program. An unstated motif throughout Sebald's essay appears to be a polemical claim for his own quasi-documentary aesthetic as the only responsible way to contemplate the bitter truth of historical memory.

5. Sebald, *Natural History of Destruction*, 51.

6. One of five hallucinatory "dreams of an insomniac" that make up the book's spiraling trajectory is the novella-length *Unmögliche Beweisaufnahme*, which was translated into English as *The Impossible Proof*, trans. Michael Lebeck (Farrar, Straus & Giroux, 1968). The same publisher put out two other novels by Nossack: *The D'Arthez Case*, trans. Michael Lebeck (1971), and *To the Unknown Hero*, trans. Ralph Manheim (1969).

Generally they spoke little about their past.
They were not given to telling stories,
and it seemed that they tried
not to think about earlier times at all.

DOSTOYEVSKY, THE HOUSE OF THE DEAD

THE END

THE END

I experienced the destruction of Hamburg as a spectator. I was spared the fate of playing a role in it. I don't know why. I can't even decide whether that was a privilege. I have talked to many hundreds of those who were there, men and women; what they have to tell, if they talk about it at all, is so unimaginably terrible that it is difficult to understand how they survived it. But they were given their role and their cue and had to act accordingly; and what they are able to report, heartwrenching though it may be in itself, is always just the part they were prompted to play. After all, most of them, as they ran out of their burning houses, didn't know that the whole city was burning. They thought it was just their street or, at most, their district, and perhaps that was what saved them.

For me the city went to ruin as a whole, and my danger consisted in being overpowered by seeing and knowing the entirety of its fate.

I feel that I have been given a mandate to render an account. Let no one ask me why I presume to speak of a mandate: I cannot answer that. I feel that my mouth would remain closed forever if I did not take care of this first. Also, I feel an urgency to set it down right away, even though only three months have passed. For reason will never be capable of comprehending as a reality or preserving in memory what happened there. I am afraid that, if I do not bear witness now, it will gradually fade like an evil dream.

On July 21, 1943, a Wednesday, I took the bus early in the morning to Horst near Maschen, a village in the heath with weekend colonies about fifteen kilometers due south of the outskirts of Hamburg. Misi had gone there the day before and had called me in the evening to tell me that she had finally succeeded in renting a small cabin for fourteen days; after how many weeks of fruitless trying and begging! And even now only because she had offered a quarter of a pound of coffee in return for the place. It was the first time in five years that I had left Hamburg for a vacation. There is no explanation for the fact that I didn't say no this time as well; for everything spoke against this vacation—if nothing else, my morbid disinclination to leave the city and my room and squander precious time, as I put it, before I had achieved something tangible.

Misi picked me up at the bus stop. She had on a red linen dress and a white head scarf. She was glad and also surprised that I had come. On the way to the cabin she tried quickly to

THE END

describe everything to me so that I wouldn't be disappointed. We still had ten more minutes to walk. Since we had to bring our own food, my luggage was quite heavy, and I complained more than was necessary. We have often thought back on that; if we had been able to look just four days ahead I would have gladly carried three times the weight without grumbling. We walked this stretch, a wide and beautiful path through the heath, scored by many sandy wheel tracks, several times a day for two months, carrying heavy loads back and forth. Once even seven hundredweights of briquettes on a small handcart.

The cabin lay to the right of the path on the ridge of a hill, hidden away among birches, evergreen bushes, and a completely neglected vegetable garden. Only the pointed red roof jutted out above. To the north there was an open view onto a treeless moorland hollow, which in turn was gently closed off by another wave of hills. Behind that the landscape descended gradually toward the Elbe and Hamburg. On a clear day you could see the towers of the city.

The owner, a mason, had built the brick cabin with his own hands. You went in through a small glass porch, not without difficulty, as it was crammed full with various tools, and entered the kitchen from there. Next came a somewhat larger living room and, adjoining it, a tiny cell that seemed to have been built at a later date, just large enough for a bed. That was to be my bedroom. There was a stairway leading from the kitchen to the attic, and there stood a second bed for Misi.

The rooms seemed even smaller than they actually were because they had been filled with completely unsuitable petit bourgeois furniture. Under the stairway was a storage bin inhabited by a small brown field mouse. Sometimes when we sat eating at the table, it would stick its little head through a crack and test the terrain with knowing eyes. But most important: in the kitchen was a trap door with an iron ring for a handle. If you lifted it, you could squeeze your way down into the cellar by means of a steep flight of stairs. It was cold there; it smelled of damp earth. The trap door and the cellar immediately reminded us of Barlach's play *The Dead Day.*

There was no light in the house; we had brought along what was left of a thick votive candle. Water had to be fetched from the neighbor's well, which was very far away. We gathered wood and pinecones in the forest every day. The stove drew very poorly and swallowed a great deal of fuel; it took an hour to get a pot of water to boil. All these inconveniences didn't disturb us then, it was all part of taking a vacation. Every time I made a fire I would run outside to watch with great pleasure the smoke billowing from my own chimney.

The first two days we had a headache, as usual, from the heath air. Then we got used to it. Except for when we went shopping in the village we hardly saw anyone. The nearest dwelling—a completely dilapidated cottage—wasn't very far off, however. The people who lived there had a bad reputation; the man was said to have spent time in jail for violating his

THE END

daughter. All the children had been found guilty of prostitution and theft and had been sent to reform schools. After the catastrophe one of the daughters was allowed to go home for several days. You could hear her singing in the heath whenever she sensed a man was near. In the evening, the mother left the house to cut grass. On her way, she would sometimes stop at our garden gate for a moment. With the shrill voice of a madwoman she would then shout something in our direction that we could only half understand. Once she gave us a cucumber, we didn't know why. Hitched to a wooden cart, her big black dog waited and watched us closely. At night he often woke us with his barking. While the woman cut grass, she let her two young goats run free; one of them kept wandering off into our garden, where it would cry like a child. Once a buck made a frightening appearance. It was huge, like a prehistoric beast.

When our primitive household wasn't taking up our attention, we sat outside and read the adventure novels we had found in the cabin. We had not brought any books; that too was part of taking a vacation. We were dressed in our oldest clothes. Above all, we had left our good shoes at home, because the heather would ruin them. We greatly regretted this precaution later on.

We watched titmice hanging on the stems of withered poppies and opening their capsules. We contested another bird's claim to the raspberries and the last cherries, which it carried from the tree to the stone gatepost to pick out the seeds there; the post was all bloody from the juice. Hawks stood in the sky, and jays scolded in the squat, earthbound oaks. In the evening a cow's cries reached us from a distant pasture, accusing and helpless.

It was the first summer weather of the year, but with it came that heat that would contribute to the ruin of Hamburg, although later it was also of some help to the homeless refugees. The heath was just beginning to bloom. Little bunches of bellflowers stood by the sides of the roads. On that hollowed slope to the north of us, some plant whose name we did not know had taken seed among the heather. It blooms in rose-colored umbels and afterward bears a mane of white cotton; since it grows almost a meter high, its blossoms floated like a rosy mist above the hollow. All that was heavy lay hidden behind a lovely unreality.

We love the heath, somehow we belong there, perhaps we were born there ages ago. Others feel sick there and become melancholy. They cannot live without time; for the heath is without time. They don't want to know that we were born of a fairy tale and will become a fairy tale again.

We began to forget the war. —

I have described this idyll on the other side of the abyss so precisely because perhaps a way can be found leading back from there to the past we have lost.

Sometime late Saturday night or Sunday morning Misi woke me up. She was calling from upstairs: "Don't you hear it?

THE END

Wouldn't you rather get up?" I had slept through the alarm; in the heath, it is only when the direction of the wind is favorable that you hear the sirens caterwauling in the far-off villages. Besides, over the years we had become used to staying in bed when the alarms sounded and not getting up until increased antiaircraft fire suggested that an actual attack was at hand; a habit that cost many people their lives.

I was about to give an irritated reply and turn over on my side when I heard it. I jumped out of bed and ran barefoot out of the house, into this sound that hovered like an oppressive weight between the clear constellations and the dark earth, not here and not there but everywhere in space; there was no escaping it.

In the northwest the hills on either side of the Elbe stood silhouetted against the narrow twilight of the departed day. The landscape cowered, holding its breath. Not far away stood a searchlight; commands were being shouted that immediately lost all connection with the earth and scattered in the void. Nervously the searchlight scanned the sky; sometimes it met with other shafts that were also swinging to and fro in wide arcs, so that for a moment they formed geometrical figures and tentlike structures, then quickly, as if startled, flew apart. It was as if this sound between heaven and earth were sucking up their light and driving them senseless. But the stars shone as they do in peacetime, straight through the invisible calamity.

One didn't dare to inhale for fear of breathing it in. It was the sound of eighteen hundred airplanes approaching Hamburg from the south at an unimaginable height. We had already experienced two hundred or even more air raids, among them some very heavy ones, but this was something completely new. And yet there was an immediate recognition: this was what everyone had been waiting for, what had hung for months like a shadow over everything we did, making us weary. It was the end. This sound was to last an hour and a half, and then again on three nights of the following week. It hung steadily in the air, and remained steady even when the much louder din of the defense intensified to a drumfire. Only at moments when individual squadrons descended for a strafing did it swell and graze the earth with its wings. And yet this terrible noise was so permeable that every other sound could be heard as well: not just the reports of the antiaircraft guns, the bursting of grenades, the howling roar of bombs, the singing of shrapnel, no, even a very soft rustling, no louder than that of a withered leaf dropping from branch to branch, and for which there was no explanation in the darkness.

The sound immediately drove me back into the house. It is possible that Misi called out to me from above, and that I answered something or other—I no longer remember. It wouldn't have been more than a few words; for this sound made a lie of all talk, it disarmed every word and pressed it to the ground. It was half an hour after midnight. The windows

THE END

of the cabin couldn't be shaded; we got dressed in the dark and kept bumping into furniture. Then Misi came downstairs with the two suitcases. I lifted the trapdoor, squeezed through the opening and climbed down the steps until only my head was above ground level. Misi handed me the two suitcases and who knows what else, and I carried everything down. In the cellar I bumped into a shelf; a glass bowl that didn't belong to us fell down and broke. The sound was already in the cellar too, yes, it may have been even louder there, the walls vibrated from it; the ground carries sounds far in the heath. We lit the votive candle, which we had placed inside a small flowerpot. I believe Misi extinguished it soon, to preserve it. I ignored the plea in her question: Wouldn't you rather stay down here too? I left her sitting there, alone on a little footstool, wrapped in blankets. I climbed back up and closed the trapdoor above her. Or maybe Misi closed it herself, thinking she would be safer that way. But safe from what? And how separate we became by setting those thin boards between us! All this is senseless, and thinking about it fills one with infinite pity for all creatures, and one falls silent because the words threaten to become sobs. Even today we are still unable to listen to music, we have to stand up and go away. When I say music I mean Bach's Air or something like that. There is something consoling in it, but it is precisely this consolation that makes us feel naked and helpless, at the mercy of a force that wants to destroy us. During those nights I walked back and forth on the narrow strip between the vegetable garden and the wire fence that enclosed the plot; there the view was unobstructed toward the north. Sometimes I stumbled over a molehill; once I fell down because my foot had got caught in the raspberry bushes.

There wasn't much for the eye to see, and it was always the same. It's not the most important thing, either. Numerous flares hung in the air above Hamburg; they were popularly known as Christmas trees. Sometimes ten, sometimes just two or one, and if at some point there were none at all, you would begin to draw hope that perhaps it was over—until new ones were dropped. Many disintegrated as they sank, and it looked as if glowing drops of metal were dripping from the sky onto the cities. In the beginning, you could follow these flares until they extinguished themselves on the ground; later they vanished in a cloud of smoke that was lit red from below by the burning city. The cloud of smoke grew from minute to minute and gradually crept eastward. I paid no attention, as I had during previous raids, to the direction of the searchlights and the focal points of the antiaircraft fire. The tracers of small-caliber antiaircraft guns were just barely visible, and the heavy artillery shells were exploding everywhere. Only when the fire was right above me and the whistling of shrapnel and the smacking sound of its impact came close did I step under the roof of the porch. A few airplanes caught fire and fell like meteors into the dark. But this didn't arouse a hunter's interest the way it used to. Where they crashed, the landscape lit up for minutes. Once the silhouette

THE END

of a distant windmill stood out against one such white incandescence. There was no feeling of cruel satisfaction at the defeat of an enemy. I remember that on one such occasion some women on the roof of a neighbor's house clapped their hands, and how at the time I angrily thought of the words with which Odysseus forbade the old nurse to rejoice over the death of the Suitors:

> Old woman, rejoice in silence; restrain yourself, and do not make any noise about it; it is an unholy thing to vaunt over dead men.

But now was no longer the time for such petty distinctions as that between friend and foe. And suddenly everything was submerged in the milky light of the netherworld. A searchlight behind me was sweeping the earth at ground level. Frightened, I turned around, and then I saw that even nature had risen up in hatred against herself. Two trunkless pines had broken through the peaceful trance of their existence and turned into black wolves avidly leaping after the bloody sickle of the moon, which was rising before them. Their eyes gleamed white and foam dripped from their snarling mouths.

I, who was walking back and forth somewhere in the void, physically, without the strength of a single thought, was I not acquainted with this hatred? Had I not kept watch over it for decades and labored to forestall its eventual explosion? Did I not know that it would burst forth some day, and did I not also yearn for this day, because it would finally relieve me of the watchman's duty? Yes, I have always known, as I know now, that the fate of the city would be my own fate. And if indeed I invoked the fate of the city in order to force my own fate to a decision, then I must stand and confess my part in the city's destruction.

We all entertained the idea of an apocalypse. The events of our time suggested it. Didn't that already mean abandoning the past? And what boastfulness was still involved, so much sophisticated chatter; for if we had seriously asked ourselves what it was that we hoped to save for those who would survive tomorrow's apocalypse, where was there anything that we would have deemed so indispensable that we would have given our last breath to preserve it? What was there that we believed in so strongly that the powers of destruction would shy away from touching this faith, so as not to bestow eternal life on what they were destroying? What was there among all the things that we used and that burdened us that was still ours? Today, I dare to cast doubt on the sincerity of those who warned us of the impending disaster and called for preparation. Is it not possible that they wished for a catastrophe so that they could force others to their knees, while they themselves felt at home in chaos? And were they not driven by the desire to test themselves, but at the cost of our familiar existence?

During all the earlier raids I had an unequivocal wish: Let it get really bad! So unequivocal that I almost want to say, I shouted it out to the heavens. It was not courage that prevented me

THE END

from ever going to the cellar but instead kept me spellbound on the balcony of my apartment. It was curiosity. Each time, I wondered: Will my wish be fulfilled? I am not saying this to give myself airs by making strange pronouncements. I believe I am obligated to express something that I suspect was felt by countless men, except that they were not conscious of it and wouldn't admit it if they were. Some will come and say: That's how it always is, and this is what it means to be male: we have to destroy in order to create. But what if the earth were to say: I gave birth to you because I longed to be more than earth. Where now is your deed? — Then we will no longer have the power to wish like that Indian, the last of his tribe, who sat by the shore of the sea and cried, What shall I do now? Shall I become Orion?

Since we no longer believe in ourselves, what are we still? Hollowed out by a night of depravity. So let's not speak of upright gait and creating!

But now the hatred was outside me, and I was free of it. I staggered on the shore of the ruined world, and a groan went through me: Oh God? Oh God! so loud that Misi heard it despite the raging destruction and called out to me from under the earth. And then I ran to her for a moment and said: This is unbearable. We leaned against each other, just lightly, shy of letting our impotence become any more apparent. Like two horses harnessed together, when one of them lays its head on the neck of its companion and then both shake off that brief tenderness with seeming annoyance. I ran out again and left

Misi alone. Wouldn't it have been better if I had sat next to her in the dark cellar, and by sharing a little body warmth we would have dreamed up a refuge from the storm? Or I would have told her a fairy tale to draw a rainbow across the abyss where the road through the hated past came to an end, a fairy tale that begins like this: Tomorrow, when it's all over... Whatever was done or not done by human beings during those nights was done or not done out of impotence.

Around 1:30 the punishment was over. From an unreal distance the all-clear signal reached our ears, so intimidated, as if it didn't dare to expect anyone to believe the lie. The northern sky was red as if after a sunset. On the nearby highway, the sirens of fire engines came howling to the rescue from neighboring cities. And with them there began a ceaseless traffic on all the streets of the region, by day and by night, an aimless flight from Hamburg. It was a river for which there was no bed; almost soundless, but inexorable, it flooded everything, and this restlessness trickled through small rivulets into the most remote villages. Sometimes someone would grasp a branch or think he had found a shore, but after a few days or hours, he would throw himself back into the river to let himself be swept further on. None of these people knew they were carrying their restlessness with them like a disease, and everything that was touched by it lost its stability.

During the second or third night raid—I am jumping ahead here—a munitions train caught fire and exploded until far

THE END

into the morning. And during the last of those nights the raging of the world against itself intensified beyond human imagination. Just before the raid a heavy thundercloud had descended over the Elbe valley and begun to discharge at the moment of the alarm, as if it had understood the sirens to be the city's final howl of anguish: Put an end to me. Presumably the raid was intended for the remaining quarter of Hamburg. But the attackers could not find their target beneath the thunderstorm and blindly dropped their bombs wherever they would fall. You could no longer tell what was thunder and lightning or bombs or artillery. Farmsteads leapt into flames all around, and the heath began to burn. The earth writhed in agony. We were afraid that the cabin would collapse. Misi came out to where I was, and we threw ourselves into the heather. And then we stumbled through the darkness toward some place where we hoped to find other people.

After a brief, paralyzing sleep we got up on Sunday morning. The sun was just rising above the two pines. The titmice were chirping, and the little cherry thief was still alive too. We lit the stove and took a table and chairs outside to eat breakfast. From north to east, over a third of the horizon was covered with smoke like black cotton. We didn't look at it. We didn't talk about the night. We didn't want to concede more weight to a dream than it deserved. After all, we were on vacation.

Then a man rode by on a bicycle. We called out to him, and he leaned against the garden gate. We showered him with questions. He was coming from Hamburg; I no longer know what he told us, it's not really important. In those first days it wasn't possible to get reliable information; the stories that were told were never accurate in their details. It was the same with me when I went there later on and people asked me when I came back: Is this and that house still there? Was the street hit too? and I was unable to give an answer; not even when I knew I must have been on that street and passed that house. One would have to have gone with the sole intention of searching for a certain address to say something accurate about it. And even then, one might have forgotten one's intention on the way. The very contradictoriness of the reports established the magnitude of the disaster beyond any doubt; the horror of it made it hard to take note of details.

Strewn across the heath lay thin strips of tin foil that were blackened on one side. It was these that had caused the rustling sound during the night, but no one knew what they were for. People warned against touching them, since they could have been poisonous. Only later did we learn that the strips had been dropped in order to prevent the defense from using radar to locate the planes. There were leaflets, too. People picked them up, read a few lines, and threw them away, bored. These leaflets contained mathematical proof of why Germany had to lose the war. What meaning did numbers still have?

Every hour a new alarm was sounded, but there wasn't another raid until noon. But what had this to do with the horror

THE END

of the night? It was almost lovely to look at. It was like gazing into a clear blue sea, and, just as if someone had thrown something into it, little clouds rose from its depths and traced a dotted trail that gradually shifted diagonally past Hamburg from the northwest. Right above us it diverged at a right angle, as if changing its mind, and strove back toward the city. And then you could see them at the head of the trail, tiny animalcules in the blue depths, silvery, glinting in the sun. They swam ahead, unswerving, obedient to some instinct. Not singly, but as if firmly connected to one another and strung into configurations that were being drawn forward by invisible threads. There were eight or ten such squadrons, and I believed I had counted thirty individual entities in each. And these configurations were in turn surrounded by nimble white worms, like dolphins gaily sporting around a ship. That was the attackers' fighter escort. — The raid lasted no longer than a quarter of an hour. Dark mushroom-shaped clouds of smoke rose out of Hamburg; the oil depots in the harbor had been hit. On Monday the spectacle was repeated.

We went to the village several times to see if there were any new developments. There was great perplexity among the people. Already during the night and at daybreak the first refugees had arrived. Some of them barefoot and in their nightshirts, just as they had leapt from their beds and run into the street. They brought with them an uncanny silence. No one dared to question these mute figures seated by the edge of the road.

Just wanting to offer them help seemed too loud an action. Then trucks arrived. The people on top of them were crouched and remote. Where are we going? Why are we stopping? Why don't you let us sleep some more? Their hands clutched bundles of incomprehensible belongings like a final weight that kept them on the ground. No lamenting anywhere, no tears. Without a word they stepped off and let themselves be led away. Only a small ugly dog leapt cheerfully off its mistress's lap and ran yapping to the nearest tree.

The people giving them shelter tried to be just as quiet and sparing in words. It must be said that the population's readiness to help was genuine beyond expectation. And not just near the city, but even further away. Not until reaching southern Germany did the refugees encounter open reluctance; at least that was the general rumor. But it may be that the people of Hamburg just didn't understand the different way of life there. I infer this from the sarcastic bitterness with which those who returned ridiculed the food, the living conditions, and the alien faith of the southerners.

But even where we were, the good relations changed in the course of a week. I am not speaking of cases where the refugees encroached on their hosts or made outrageous demands. There were those, to be sure, but many took this position: We have lost everything, now please give us half of what you have! and laid their hands in their laps. And on the opposite side there were enough people who thought: It's not our fault, so what business

THE END

is it of ours? And when they gave anything, it was out of fear. This pitiful fact—that those who were spared felt envied from the beginning—may very well have lit and then fanned the spark of envy in the refugees. And though this may be hard to believe, a point was reached when the refugees were begrudged the few new things they had received as gifts or as allocations from the State. Or else—but it is only now that I ask this question—could there have been a deeper reason? Did those who had been forced to hazard the leap into nothingness become objects of envy because they had already gone through the ordeal that was awaiting everyone else?

There began a time without masks; the familiar disguises dropped off of their own accord, as had occurred to the two pine trees during the night. Greed and fear exposed themselves without shame and suppressed all tender feeling. We all had to recognize during those weeks that the scales we had used for weighing were no longer accurate. Those nearest to us or those whom we called friends either kept complete silence or evaded their duty with a few shabby words about the hard times that made it impossible for them to help. The concept of kinship completely broke down. Ask a hundred people today, regardless of their class and whether they suffered losses or not, ninety-nine will answer with a dismissive grimace: Better a stranger than a relative! It is a fact, so let it be stated as such, without bitterness and without drawing hasty conclusions. Instead, let us hold to the heartening experience of seeing those who had been most distant, sometimes the most fleeting acquaintances, or business associates, step into the breach without hesitation and with such kindness that one is shamed into asking oneself whether one would have done the same if the situation were reversed.

But even the most generous hand can become tired of giving, and it is even more difficult to learn to let oneself be the recipient of gifts and to receive, always and only to receive, without thereby losing one's freedom. But does this sufficiently explain why such discord arose so quickly? No. I believe, rather, that people expected something entirely different of each other, something of which they were not capable. Who can blame the helpers for being disappointed when they had to realize that what they had offered—shelter, food, and clothing—basically didn't make any difference at all? Perhaps something like pleasure flitted across the recipients' faces, but it didn't linger. They would walk through the strange rooms, touch an object, hold it, and look at it absently. The host would follow them with his eyes and expect some statement like: We, too, once had something like this—and perhaps then he would have given it to them. But instead, the stranger would put it aside, and the unspoken question would fill the room: What is the use of still having such things? It would have been easier to assuage loud lamentation. It is very probable that such laments were expected, or at least a forced self-composure indicative of suppressed tears. Those who were known

THE END

to have experienced unimaginably frightful hours, who had run through fire with their clothes burning, stumbling over charred corpses; before whose eyes and in whose arms children had suffocated; who had seen their houses collapsing right after their father or husband had gone back inside to save something or other; all those who had spent months hoping for news from the missing and who at the very least had lost all their possessions in a matter of minutes—why didn't they cry and lament? And why this indifferent tone of voice when they spoke of what they had left behind, this dispassionate manner of talking, as if telling about a terrible event from prehistoric times that would be impossible today, that is almost forgotten except for the shockwaves that still faintly agitate our dreams? And then this muffled voice, impervious to daylight, and so timid, the way one speaks at night, outside, when one doesn't know where there might be an ear secretly listening.

And what did the victims expect when they seemed to accept all the good that was done to them merely to please the givers? The instinct of the helpers rebelled; not only because their gift was robbed of its value, but also because they themselves were robbed of all security and began to have doubts about their own possessions.

I now dare to give an answer to that question. We expected someone to call out to us: Wake up! It was just a bad dream! But we couldn't ask for that, the nightmare closed our mouths to the point of suffocation. And how could anyone have awakened us?

So it came to pass that people who lived together in the same house and ate at the same table breathed the air of completely separate worlds. They tried to reach out to each other, but their hands did not meet. Which of them, then, was blind? They spoke the same language, but what they meant by their words were entirely different realities. Which of them, then, was deaf? We have still found no way to translate this to each other. There are those who say by their actions: See, life goes on. Despite everything! We hear it and nod: Yes, that's true, we know it from the way it used to be. And then one of us will in turn try to explain himself, perhaps like this: Imagine closing your eyes for a second, and when you open them again, nothing is left of what was there before. Immediately the one who is listening misunderstands it and thinks we are mourning for people we have lost and for things we must now do without, or else he will think we are talking about monetary value or middle-class comfort. He will try to console us by telling us that some things at least can be replaced. But that's not it at all. Perhaps then we will try to speak of a lost atmosphere, and that, too, will be misunderstood. Eventually we become impatient and unfair with the listener. Or else we're ashamed of talking about it too much and give up. Would it be better understood if it were told at dusk as a fairy tale? There once was a creature that was not born of a mother. A fist struck it naked into the world, and a voice called: Fend for yourself! Then it opened its eyes and didn't know what to make of its

THE END

surroundings. And it didn't dare to look back, for behind it there was nothing but fire.

We no longer have a past. Perhaps we would not feel this so painfully if there were not people who still have a past from which they derive their standard for tomorrow. And they seem to be the stronger ones, so we really should follow their example. Oh, what a fruitless effort it is to make their goal our own! And so the world is divided into two parts, and between them lies an invisible abyss that both sides are aware of. The people on either side have begun to hate each other, without wanting to and without any fault of their own, although each would like to hold the other responsible. How often, when I ask one of the victims about someone who I know was their friend, do I hear the answer: He's finished for me.

We have had more than one occasion to experience the frightening extent to which we have lost touch with everything we once took for granted. When Misi and I walked through our ruined district looking for our street, we saw inside a house that stood alone and intact in the midst of a vast expanse of rubble a woman cleaning her windows. We nudged each other, we stood still as if spellbound. We thought this was a madwoman. The same thing happened when we saw children cleaning and raking a small front yard. That was so incomprehensible that we told others about it as if it were God knows what. And one afternoon we arrived at a completely undestroyed suburb. People were sitting on their balconies drinking coffee.

It was like a movie, it wasn't really possible. I don't know what detours of reason led us to the realization that we were observing these actions through inverted eyes. Then in turn we were shocked at ourselves.

We found out on Tuesday morning that we had lost everything. Misi had gone to the Mayor's office to ask for ration cards, since the mail she had expected from Hamburg hadn't arrived. There she met a soldier who had lived in our neighborhood and whose family had become refugees—he was hoping to find them in Maschen. He told Misi that the house our apartment was in was no longer standing. I hadn't gone with her; I was sitting in the garden trying to read a book. Stepping through the garden gate, Misi said: Yes, now it's finally happened. That was all, and even later we didn't talk much about it. We both behaved as if we had known it all along. It took half an hour to get from the Mayor's office to our cabin. I ask myself today what Misi was thinking during that half hour, and it frightens me that she was alone.

We wanted to go to Hamburg the very next day, a Wednesday. Then the next raid came during the night, and we postponed it till Thursday. And then from Thursday till Friday, I no longer remember why. And since there was another raid on Thursday night, we stayed put on Friday as well. We didn't rouse ourselves for the trip until Saturday. Going to Hamburg wasn't easy, by the way, since the trains weren't running. Also,

THE END

the wildest rumors were circulating: supposedly, plagues had broken out in Hamburg, and no one was allowed to cross the Elbe bridge. Or the other way around: you wouldn't be let back out, anyone capable of working was being assigned to rescue operations. None of this conformed to the facts, or it was only half true. Still, it was not inconceivable, and the few official announcements that arrived from the city were full of contradictions. But all this was really just a pretext for us, a form of cowardice that we indulged in: we were willing to accept any excuse to postpone the moment when we would have to look fate in the eye. We tried hard, during this interval, to behave as if nothing had happened. We told ourselves that every day, every hour was an opportunity, a gift we would never be offered again. But how difficult it was to maintain this deception. Every five minutes it was pierced by a sigh from one of us. Nothing could hinder our thoughts from going to Hamburg. Then, when we asked ourselves what it was that had crossed our minds, it always turned out to be some trivial, ordinary thing. Not, as one might have suspected, something precious, irreplaceable; such things did not, for the time being, play any role, they even seemed to have been forgotten. And among these trivial things it was again those we happened to have used shortly before we left home. There was a perfectly ordinary deckchair for the balcony. On the previous Sunday we had re-covered it with material from a window awning. I don't know how often we bumped into this deckchair with our thoughts and halted in front of it. I believe that at the time this was our greatest danger. We very nearly stumbled over it and could have fallen into the abyss.

The moment we received the news, we became refugees. So it made no difference that chance had allowed us to escape a few days before the catastrophe. Whether we wanted to or not, we were drawn to our kind and even felt shy with the others. The refugees, by the way, were all very simple people, but no one took notice of such things; our common fate made us equal. Nor did anyone talk about having lost more than another, at least not during the first days. We weren't weighing and judging yet, the irreplaceable was at issue; for whatever can be expressed in numbers can be replaced. But a unique work of art or a faded photograph or an old doll from one's childhood, what does all this have to do with numbers? These things have their life from us, because at some time we bestowed our affection on them; they absorbed our warmth and harbored it gratefully in order to enrich us with it again in meager hours. We were responsible for them; they could only die with us. And now they stood on the other side of the abyss in the fire and cried after us, begging: Don't leave us! We knew it, we heard it, and dared not pronounce their names, because pity would have destroyed us. We could not even dare to look back at them. We expected their voices to grow fainter the further we moved away from the fire, but they did not let us forsake them. If we had known, back then, that this torment would grow from

THE END

week to week and that we would speak more and more quietly and would find ourselves halting in midsentence because the voices confused us, we would have thought ourselves fortunate to be able to perish with them right away. Oh, and how often one hears this said nowadays!

The most dangerous thing was the words "could have." It required a painful vigilance not to say "could have." I once walked past two women sitting by the ditch on the side of the road with their backs turned toward me. It was a grandmother with her grown daughter; some children may have been playing nearby. I only heard the old woman's words: Didn't I always tell you, you could have—and at that point the daughter howled like a mortally wounded animal. And nowadays, when someone in conversation is on the verge of straying into the realm of "could have," someone else will quickly admonish or beg him to stop; or the speaker will notice it himself and abruptly break off, saying: Oh well, it doesn't matter.

I keep using the word "abyss," and maybe someone will feel this is an exaggeration. But then that person cannot imagine what danger we were in. It was a hundred times greater than the danger of fire and bombs; for there was no escaping it. And we knew that. The abyss was nearby, right next to us, or even beneath us, and we were just hovering above it thanks to some kind of grace. The only thing we could do was not to be loud and not to weigh too much. All any one of us would have had to do was scream, and we would all have been lost.

That is one reason why the refugees anxiously watched out for each other, lest anyone lose his composure. It was also more the way animals huddle together for warmth. We were all strangely and randomly dressed; some were walking around in silk dresses, others looked like vagabonds. But no one had eyes for that. Except that, even though it was only the end of July and scorching hot, we were already afraid of the winter. We had no beds, no blankets, no coats, no warm underwear, and above all, no shoes. Suddenly we thought we had come to the realization that these things were the only necessities of life. We passed on this new insight to friends in urgently worded letters: Drop everything else! Just keep your winter clothes and solid shoes!

Occasionally we also talked about how to approach the authorities that had promised us aid and restitution, but without eagerness or faith in the possibility of such aid, at least at the beginning. Whenever one of us mentioned something like that, the others would listen with anxious expectation, and this in turn would make the speaker uncertain, as if he had already said too much. Others devoted themselves with emphatic zeal to various necessary tasks. They washed clothes, ran around shopping for this and that, peeled vegetables, and so forth, tightlipped and sullen. But then, without any external prompting, they would suddenly drop everything and go off where people were standing together, and listen, completely forgetting their half-finished chores. To an uninvolved observer

THE END

it must have looked as if we had a lot of time; but actually we were driven. We didn't have much time; indeed, we no longer had any time at all, we were outside of time. Everything we did immediately lost its meaning. As soon as we eagerly followed some hopeful train of thought, a tenacious fog would envelop us, and we would sit back down by the side of the road, disheartened.

But the visage of man in those days—who would dare to forget it. The eyes had grown larger and transparent, as they appear in icons. The cold, meanly divisive window glass was shattered, and through the wide openings the infinite behind man wafted unhindered into the endlessness before him and hallowed his countenance for the passage of what is beyond time. Let us cast this visage as a constellation into the sky, to remind us of our last chance before everything turns into a faceless mass. Naturally there came the day when this paralysis of the will was recognized as a disease. The refugees were to be forcibly transported to southern Germany to relieve the surroundings of Hamburg of their presence. Many submitted to these ordinances; some got off the trains on the way and struggled on unassisted; others hid or managed somehow to delay their deportation. Misi and I suddenly called out to each other: Refugees! We can't let that happen! What that word meant to us was a creature who had completely surrendered itself to the authorities and their plans. But the pain of tearing oneself loose can hardly be described. Again and again one was seized by the current, always in danger of being swept into some weary morass. It was like a dream where you want to escape but your feet won't obey your will. The pursuer is coming close and you feel paralyzed.

We suddenly began to loathe our cabin. Gathering wood, fetching water, the bad beds, the stove that wouldn't draw, all the flaws that were part and parcel of a vacation retreat now seemed unbearable, because we might have to face spending the winter and who knows how many seasons there. Chance offered us another shelter, not far away. A lady agreed to put us up in her house for a fee. We moved in with her in the middle of August and no longer needed to provide for our meals. When we entered the modern, well-appointed rooms, how greatly improved our situation seemed! After a few hours, though, we noticed that we were no longer alone and had thus waived our rights to the principal advantage the cabin had offered us. If we had only known where to go, we would have moved on after two days. Instead our aimlessness brought unrest into another home. —

It wasn't until Saturday, then, that we finally went to Hamburg. That was before the last raid, which took place on Monday. The trip to Hamburg proceeded as follows: on the highway you would stop a truck on which you expected to find a vacant seat, and take the ride for as long as was convenient. Then you would wait for another vehicle, and in this way, changing from car to car, you would get to the city fairly quickly. Cars from all over the country had been requisitioned for this service. Later, when the trains were running and automobile

THE END

traffic was discontinued again, it took much longer, about four hours each way for that short distance. At the train station in Maschen, when the train finally arrived from Lüneburg, you had to fight for a seat, and in Harburg once again. People climbed in through the windows and hung onto the sides of the trains like grapes. When you finally arrived you were completely exhausted.

Countless numbers of people traveled like this every day. I have the impression that, by and large, these trips were by no means necessary, be it to salvage something or to go on a search for relatives, or for business reasons. But neither would I claim that it was mere curiosity. People were simply without a center; the roots were torn out and swayed back and forth in search of some soil, and everyone was afraid of missing something. Or else it was simply the force that drives a murderer back to the scene of his crime.

I have spoken with several thousand people. The conversations always revolved around the same subject: Where did you live? Did you lose everything too? On which night did it happen? Where are you staying now? And what's going to happen now? — We were without exception firmly convinced that the war would be over very shortly; no one argued this point at all; for us, after all, the die was already cast. There remained only the question of how and in what place of refuge we would be able to weather this brief interval.

No one thought any further than that then. The slogan that only victory could compensate for our losses was not issued until later, and was partly accepted by the masses. But during those days, if by chance a newspaper came into our hands, we didn't bother to read the war bulletins; we didn't even understand why they were being released. We would immediately turn to the page with the announcements that concerned us directly. Whatever happened outside of us simply did not exist. Our fate was decided, it couldn't be changed by any event in the rest of the world. This attitude led us to make many mistakes. But time will tell whether we weren't fundamentally right. It's true that several months have passed and other cities have been destroyed in the same way, but Hamburg was the first big city to be annihilated. We may have received the mortal wound, and what follows are merely death throes. If we disregard the war and the fact that one or the other side could win it, if we only think of our homeland, Europe, then it was doubtless correct that we felt our fate to be the end.

It would be a mistake, however, to speak of latent unrest and rebellion at the time. Not only the enemies but also our own authorities miscalculated in this respect. Everything went on very quietly and with a definite concern for order, and the State took its bearings from this order that had arisen out of the circumstances. Wherever the State sought to impose regulations of its own, people just got upset and angry. The powerful and their officials had partly vanished from the face of the earth, but wherever they still led a spurious and, as it were, tolerated existence, they would yield as soon as someone bristled in protest.

THE END

What else could they do? In the Harburg train station I heard a woman who had broken some rule or other, screaming: Go ahead, put me in jail, then at least I'll have a roof over my head! and three armed railway policemen didn't know what else to do except to slip away, embarrassed, leaving it up to the crowd to pacify the woman. I have experienced many other cases, including some that were a good deal more hostile, but this example is sufficient; it illustrates clearly our attitude and the impotence of the State. Every one of us would have said what that woman said if the State had gotten in our way.

Today the State credits itself with having exercised "restraint," but that is ridiculous. Others say we were much too apathetic at the time to be capable of revolt. That is not true either. In those days everyone said what was on his mind, and no feeling was further from people than fear. After everything I have heard, I am coming to the conclusion that no greater contempt could have been shown to what is called the State than to treat it as something completely irrelevant that could neither be blamed for a fate such as Hamburg had suffered nor be expected to do anything about it. It was a moment when man no longer showed himself to be a slave to his institutions. For example, everyone knew that precisely those whose position and whose promises should have obliged them to stay at their posts and help until the end had been the first to run away and had, on top of that, ruthlessly misused their influence to get hold of vehicles in which they carted off their belongings; yes, and that they left other refugees lying on the street with their last bundle. This is not an isolated case and not exaggerated; thousands saw it. But when people talked about it, their words, though bitter, were far from being vengeful, but rather as if laughing at themselves for ever having expected anything else. Woe to us if the powerful should take revenge some day for this contempt! But I believe they didn't even understand it.

And another thing: I have not heard a single person curse the enemies or blame them for the destruction. When the newspapers published epithets like "pirates of the air" and "criminal arsonists," we had no ears for that. A much deeper insight forbade us to think of an enemy who was supposed to have caused all this; for us, he, too, was at most an instrument of unknowable forces that sought to annihilate us. I have not met even a single person who comforted himself with the thought of revenge. On the contrary, what was commonly said or thought was: Why should the others be destroyed as well? I have been told that a man who was prattling about revenge and about exterminating the enemy with gas was beaten to a pulp. I was not present, but if it did happen, it was in order to silence a blasphemous stupidity.

All this must be said once and for all; for it redounds to the glory of man that on the day of reckoning he experienced his fate with such largeness of spirit. Even though it was just for a brief period; for in the meantime the picture has become confused again. —

THE END

On the first truck that brought us closer to Hamburg, I experienced something in myself about which I have not spoken with anyone and that fills me with a kind of shy wonder, because I don't dare to interpret it. We had found a seat for Misi on top of a vegetable crate with her back against the wall of the driver's seat, so that she was more or less protected from the draft. I stood tightly wedged among twenty or thirty people. To avoid being thrown off we hung onto the iron bars that held the canvas topping in place. Often we had to duck down to avoid being whipped by the branches of fruit trees that shadowed the street. It was close to eight in the morning, and the air was fresh and young. The corn was fully ripe. Black-and-white cows were drowsily chewing their cud on the rich marsh meadows. Here and there a foal gazed, astonished, over the top of a fence and then leapt back abruptly to tell its mother about us. And from the fertile plain, familiar colonies of oaks rose like islands, with old farmsteads hidden beneath their low branches. Sometimes a village church rose up steeply, or the baroque roof of a parsonage.

We traveled swiftly through this land of peace toward the dead city. Then there came over me, I don't know from where, a feeling of joy that was so true and compelling that I was hard put not to shout exultantly: Now at last real life begins. As if a prison door had sprung open before me and the clear air of freedom, long anticipated, were suddenly blowing in my face. It was like a fulfillment.

And yet Misi too must have felt something similar. Several times when we tried to talk about our future, she told me she had the feeling that now my last great chance was presenting itself, and that I must not miss it. Did she really just mean the paralyzing compromises we had gotten ensnared in, out of indolence or false respect, and which now no longer bound us because a higher power had severed them? Or did she mean something beyond these fetters, which, after all, are only fetters if they are experienced as such and perhaps are beneficent fetters because they deceive us about the time spent waiting for the hour of fulfillment—did Misi also mean that the terrible desert of preparation had now been traversed?

What a contradiction there was between this feeling and the facts! Or else one would have to assume that a person experiences something similar right after dying and that the last smile blossoms from that posthumous joy.

Am I just talking about a purely personal feeling? If so, it would not belong in this report. —

A little way beyond Wilhelmsburg, signs of destruction began to appear, and on the Veddel one was already confronted with the spectacle of total annihilation. Oh, as I ride back in memory down that road into Hamburg I feel the urge to stop and give up. Why go on? I mean, why record all this? Wouldn't it be better to surrender it to oblivion for all time? For those who were there certainly don't have to read it. And the others, and those who will come later? What if they read it only to enjoy

THE END

something strange and uncanny and to make themselves feel more alive? Does it take an apocalypse to do that? Or a descent into the underworld? And we who have been there do not even dare to utter a prophetic warning. Not yet!

Or is this a plea to the others that they not judge us for no longer meeting their expectations, for no longer being so responsive, so reliably ourselves? —

I don't imagine that I am rendering a first impression. That would be wrong; it is a conspicuous fact that repeated visits did not accustom or inure us to what we saw. Each time one emerged again from the haze of the city, it was like coming to after having fainted. Or one would be devastated, numb, and depleted, like a poet who has held converse with demons. Not out of grief and fright, as it used to be when we saw one house destroyed among ten left standing. For it was possible, then, to mourn for that single house torn from the midst of the living, and at the same time to tremble for the life of the others. But now, when nothing was left? Not the corpse of the city, not something known and now dead, that would speak to us: Alas, yesterday, when I still lived, I was your home—no, there was no need to mourn. What surrounded us did not remind us in any way of what was lost. It had nothing to do with it. It was something else, it was strangeness itself, it was the essentially not possible.

In northern Finland there are forests that are frozen solid. We had a picture of one hanging in our apartment. But who still thinks of a forest in the face of this? It isn't even the skeleton of a forest. Something is there, to be sure, even more than if it were only a skeleton, but what is the meaning of these signs and runes? Perhaps the inconceivable inversion of the concept "forest"?

I saw the faces of those standing next to me on the truck as we went down the broad artery across the Veddel to the Elbe bridge. We were like a group of tourists; the only thing missing was a megaphone and a guide's informational chatter. And already we were perplexed and did not know how to explain the strangeness. Where once one's gaze had hit upon the walls of houses, a silent plain now stretched to infinity. Was it a cemetery? But what sort of creatures had interred their dead there and planted chimneys on their graves? Solitary chimneys that grew from the ground like cenotaphs, like Neolithic dolmens or admonishing fingers. Did those who lay beneath inhale the ethereal blue through those chimneys? And there, among those strange shrubs, where an empty façade hung in the air like a triumphal arch, was that the resting place of one of their lords and heroes? Or were these the remains of an aqueduct such as the ancient Romans had built? Or was all this just scenery for a fantastic opera? — How many things we had learned in school, how many books we had read, how many illustrations we had marveled at, but we had never seen a report about anything like this. So there were unknown continents after all? I saw in everyone's eyes this intent watchful scanning of the outer landscape and an unavailing search for comparisons

THE END

within. This expectance of something that would appear somewhere and explain the riddle, and that it was imperative not to overlook.

Only during the brief crossing of the Elbe bridge was the spell lifted for a moment, while everyone began to count the towers of the city. Oh, and with what affectionate nicknames they were summoned, one by one! And where was the most beautiful of them all, the tower of Saint Catherine's Church? And why had the town hall turned into a pagoda? — But at that point we had already crossed the river and were driving into the cemetery.

Immediately to our left there burned a gigantic pile of coke— it didn't stop burning for three weeks—and for several seconds a hellish heat breathed in our faces, like an immunization before crossing the border, and then we were inside. The truck swayed and groped its way through the narrow makeshift passage that had been cleared among the ruins, across slopes of rubble, the vestiges of collapsed buildings, past craters and beneath bridges that had snapped in two, railroad cars dangling from them like garlands into the waters of the docks, from which the black bow of a cargo boat reared up, startled by the cumbersome bodies of barges drifting lifeless on their sides. Along the edges of the passage lay longish bundles, and people said these were corpses. All of them so quiet. How much louder in our minds was the soundless death scream of the cars that, baked to a yellow ash and writhing in ultimate agony, marked their drivers' hopeless escape route.

And no side streets into the thicket; everything was matted together. Only rarely an open view through the blackness of an arched window. And above them, instead of epitaphs, incomprehensible advertisements. Suddenly we pulled in our heads because the front of a seven-story building was leaning over the street, threatening to collapse from the vibrations of the truck. Once past it, turning around, we saw a balcony dangling way on top, and above it an open awning and even a flowerbox with red geraniums. But everything utterly silent, unmoving, unchanging. Denuded of time, it had become eternal.

From now on we can no longer ask ourselves: Will it hold its own, your work, in the presence of the wide countryside and by the edge of the sea? We will have to ask: Will it hold its own in the presence of this cemetery?

How conceited we were, how proud of our good taste! How satisfied with the cleverness of our judgment! And with what cynical disgust we presumed to reject the way countless people lived and behaved! Didn't we say: This is an ugly district, unfit for human habitation, ripe for demolition; these streets, so narrow, and everyone's yelling; these backyards without light, without color, without air; these houses, all stunted and dirty? How could millions of people live in this narrowness and not explode it with their breath? And the staircases smelled of food and of ordinary people; we turned up our noses at the thought. From the apartments, the vapors of boiling laundry blew in our faces, and the rooms looked cold with their unused furniture.

THE END

And that velveteen couch with the crocheted doilies? And all those awkward photographs of weddings and anniversaries? And the color print of saccharine nymphs hanging over the matrimonial bed?

Who would still dare to make fun of these things! Why are there no smells on the stairs any longer? Why is there no laundry drying on the rack outside the kitchen window? Didn't people sometimes bake a cake on Sunday? Wasn't there in every one of these numberless apartments, whose contours were now discernible only in what was left of the walls, a housewife who polished the floors and dusted the furniture day in, day out; who was afraid of her neighbors yet wanted to be envied by them?

And why are the chimneys still there, meaningless and without smoke? But there's no stove left. What did we cook for? And no beds, either! Why did we sleep? Why did we sustain ourselves? Why did we collect provisions and save money?

Everything that men have to say about this is a lie. It is not permissible to talk about it except in the language of women.

I have gone through all these districts, by foot or by car. Only a few main streets were cleared, but mile after mile there was not a single living house. And if you tried to work your way through the ruins on either side, right away you would lose all sense of time and direction. In areas I thought I knew well, I lost my way completely. I searched for a street that I should have been able to find in my sleep. I stood where I thought it must be and didn't know which way to turn. I counted on my fingers the lateral furrows in the rubble, but I could not find the street again. And if after hours of searching you met a person, it would only be someone else wandering in a dream through the eternal wasteland. We would pass each other with a shy look and speak even more softly than before. Somewhere the sun was shining, but it had no power over this twilight.

Once I was there with a man whom at another time I would not have liked, so that I would have avoided his company. But in the way we sought to orient ourselves now, the way we tried to overlook what we saw and treat it as something self-evident about which no words need be wasted, we were exactly alike. In fact, I believe we both felt like burglars. We observed our alien surroundings with a kind of alert hostility, careful not to make a noise that could wake a sleeping person or a dog, and took fright at a torn curtain that blew from a silent verandah. Who was giving whom a sign there? Are they lying in ambush, insidious and mute, these invisible beings that must be at home in this foreign land? Or is it we who are deaf and blind? Why does it not tear through our paralysis like a boundless scream when we see written with chalk on a front door the first and last question: Where are you, Mother? Please let me know. I now live in this and that place.

We walked through the world like dead men who no longer care about the petty miseries of the living. There was an attempt to banish the dead by means of numbers. During

THE END

the very first days the number forty thousand was given. But this offended those who did not want to be counted, and the number one hundred and twenty-five was tried. Now the number took over, it grew from day to day and rose to three hundred thousand. Then one morning we woke up, and it was only thirty thousand. All the rules of logic were invoked to prove that it couldn't have been more. Someone had opened hostilities against the dead. At the same time, we heard from all parts of the Reich that things weren't all that bad in Hamburg and that the people there were just making a fuss. We were so astounded by this that we couldn't say anything in reply; for no one had yet gotten to the point of pitying himself or boasting of his misfortune. But the dead did not wish to be conquered by logic. Today the number again wavers between sixty thousand and a hundred thousand, and no one dares to object.

Why do they try to lie to the dead? Why don't they say: We can't count them! That would be a simple statement such as the dead, too, could understand. For otherwise it could be that, if they are not granted their right, they will gather one day around the monument from World War One, which was left standing along with the chimneys while three-quarters of the city were laid waste. And they will ask those for whom the inscription, "Forty thousand sons of the city gave their lives for you! 1914–1918," was written, they will ask those forty thousand: "Your parents, wives, and children, too, many and without number—tell us,

O sons, for what? In five and a half hours!" And then there will be no one who could answer. And in place of that worthless eagle chiseled by a boastful age into the monument, there will appear again the great rune of mother sorrow. — A week later, these sections of the city were completely closed off. A high wall was built around them; there certainly were enough stones. Armed guards stood at the entrance. "What are they after, anyway," one of them said to me, "this is no fun." One could see convicts in striped suits working in there. They were supposed to recover the dead. People said that the corpses, or whatever one wants to call the remains of dead people, were burned on the spot or destroyed in the cellars with flamethrowers. But actually, it was worse. The flies were so thick that the men couldn't get into the cellars, they kept slipping on maggots the size of fingers, and the flames had to clear the way for them to reach those who had perished in flames.

Rats and flies were the lords of the city. Insolent and fat, the rats disported themselves on the streets. But even more nauseating were the flies. They were large and of a shimmering green; no one had ever seen flies like this. They wallowed in swarming clumps on the pavement, sat, copulating, on top of the ruined walls, warmed themselves, bloated and tired, on splinters of window glass. When they could no longer fly, they would crawl after us through the narrowest crevices, soiling everything, and their rustling and buzzing was the first thing one heard in the morning. This didn't stop until October.

THE END

And then the smell of charred household effects, of rot and decay, hanging over the city. And this smell was visible as a dry plaster dust that was blown everywhere. A sudden craving for perfume arose in us. —

On that first day, we got off the truck near the indoor market. We wanted first to go to the free port and see what had happened to the office. We had not heard any news about it yet and hoped we would still be able to salvage something there. The area was virtually deserted, but there was less damage here than elsewhere. Half the houses had been left standing, or else only the roofs and the upper floors had burnt down. Here and there, people were poking about in the rubble or carrying a partially singed piece of furniture onto the street.

We crossed the customs canal. The customs bureau was gone. When we turned the corner near Saint Anne's, we saw the red row of counting houses. But we still couldn't tell whether these weren't just façades. Suddenly we met the first person we knew, an engineer from the warehouses. I think we talked gibberish, the words tumbled out of our mouths. It was like coming home after twenty years and running into a former playmate.

We asked him about people we knew in common, but he knew nothing about them, either. He seemed absent, by the way. I would ask something, he would say yes, and a second later it was forgotten. When he looked at you, his gaze went off somewhere into the void. He was a very polite man, he hadn't lost this quality yet, but the old politeness flapped loosely around him like an ill-fitting suit, it didn't go with his present appearance. This was all due to lack of sleep and overexertion from fighting the fires, and perhaps also due to alcohol, which he drank to keep himself going. He immediately pulled a small bottle of schnapps from his pocket and gave it to us as a present. We each took a sip from it; that bottle served us well throughout the day. Just eight days previously, who would have thought that Misi and I would be standing on the street drinking from a bottle with a man we hardly knew? But actually the concept "street" no longer existed.

He told us that Hamburg had been given up during the night. The fire brigades had been hard at work when they were recalled in the evening and left to stand idle on a side street all night. That was when he decided to stop working and finally went to sleep, even though all around him everything stood in flames. — Later his wife joined him. The apartment provided by their employer in the harbor was still intact, but they had moved all their belongings out of the city.

The counting houses had for the most part burned down to the third floor. By detours, across glass and debris, we arrived at our office. Everything had been drenched in the struggle to put out the fires. The back wall of the building had been torn open by a demolition bomb, and the corridors led directly into the canal. At the entrance to our office, the ceiling hung down to the floor like a curtain. It still hangs like that today. Inside, everything was in wild disarray: furniture, documents,

THE END

doors, and window frames. The dividing walls had been swept away, and anything you touched left splinters of glass in your hands. — But we had seen this before. In May 1941, the office had been destroyed in a similar manner.

I broke open my desk and, to my joy, found some manuscripts in it. I didn't succeed in opening the safe. Anything we considered valuable we stuffed into sacks and wrapped in an old woolen blanket. And suddenly everything was valuable: an old towel, a nailbrush, a wrought iron candlestick, and who knows what else. We moved two typewriters into a cellar that could still be locked, and decided to take a third one with us. And that was good, for during the following days the human vultures of the city filched everything that could be moved, from the smallest objects to rugs and furniture. Notices were posted everywhere saying that looters would be shot, but who was going to catch them in order to shoot them? What the mob took from our offices were mainly the small cans filled with coffee samples that had formerly stood neatly lined up on top of shelves. There were a hundred offices, and not a single coffee bean—literally—could be found after the looting.

Suddenly we hesitated; our gaze had fallen through the back window onto Saint Catherine's Church. Shocked, we looked at each other. "Yes, I cried when it caved in," said the engineer, who was standing next to us. He told us the precise hour when it had happened. It didn't help when we tried to persuade ourselves: It's just a church, what about those hundreds of thousands of homes and the people, that's so much worse. I suppose it was a symbol. All of us who had worked there loved that steeple exceedingly, each in his own way, perhaps without knowing it. We only realized it now. For more than a decade it had stood in front of my desk. The blue-green of the baroque roof enchanted the opalescent waters of the canal. Especially during the spring and fall you would find yourself drawn into reverie by the sight of it. It wasn't even necessary to know about an old organ there and that this was the only church that had survived the fire of Hamburg a hundred years earlier.

Now all that was left of the steeple was a pitifully rotted and blackened stump. It had broken off right above the clock, the hour hand was pointing to shortly after one; but was it noon or midnight? And on what date? Above the clock you could still see the word "Gloria" in gold letters. The copper of the roof had draped itself over the nave like a shroud. Only way in back, on a remnant of the sacristy, the golden saint still stood with his steering wheel, pointing a finger into the distance.

But now I remember having felt deeply disturbed some time in May of this year, when two large gull-like birds circled the church soundlessly and almost without a stroke of their wings. They were sometimes black and sometimes white, and the way their shadows slid across the houses and the water filled me with anxiety. The many hundreds of much smaller gulls interrupted their voracious activities, fell silent, ducked,

THE END

and watched the strangers with tilted heads. This happened only on one afternoon.

But we're always told we shouldn't be superstitious. —

Heavily laden, we set out for the city. We had to rest several times on the way. I believe we never looked right or left but just strove onward. I used to walk that road every day, and now again. But for how much longer? And it really isn't the same road anymore. True, they have filled in the crater in the fish market where the water kept flowing from the broken pipes, but the old pharmacy is gone, and the Johanneum school can never be rebuilt. But all this we are only aware of now, when the cleared streets and everyone's almost cynical desire to walk and live on them as in the past makes one conscious of what is missing. For back then, there were no streets, only paths across rubble and glass. And people weren't thinking of morality and order, they just walked where they could and dressed as they pleased and as was convenient. Nor was anyone surprised to see people build small fireplaces out of bricks and squat before them under the open sky as if in a jungle, boiling their food or their laundry. At least it was life. In other parts of the city there wasn't even that.

Not until we arrived at the Jungfernstieg did we succeed in stopping a doctor, who gave us a ride in his car to the university. Incidentally, it would have taken us just a few minutes out of our way to look up a friend. We felt an urge to do that, and nevertheless we didn't. Not only on that first day, but three or four other times. He could have needed our help, so there is no excuse for it. Actually we were afraid of not seeing him again. In those days people did not like to inquire after friends and relatives. It was preferable to let chance deliver the news. At least in the beginning, that is how it was.

What an effort it cost me to summon the courage to go there, finally, after eight days! Already as I was walking up the Heuberg, I almost turned back to avoid seeing the truth. It used to be narrow there, a maze of crisscrossing alleys, and now you had an open view. Around the corner of the Hohe Bleiche a large mound of rubble covered the street. I could still not make out the condition of my friend's house. Not until I climbed the barricade—and again I had to consider it for a long time, and I believe my heart was trembling—not until then did I see the house. It was so unbelievable. It clung as the first or last house on the street to the wall of another building, like a towering cliff over the petrified surf of that sea of ruins. And in front of it a single man was working, and it was him. I shouted, and he shouted, too; I leapt off the barricade and fell. We embraced with ridiculous gestures, and the red stubble of his week-old beard scratched me.

He was clearing the entrance. You had to walk on a board to get into the house. The buildings on the other side of the street had fallen against the ground floor and the basement and crushed them. The flames had blackened the house and reached in through the windows. In a nightlong struggle, he and his

THE END

wife had put out the flames again and again. But though they were able to fight the fire, it remains an inexplicable miracle that this house was the only one that withstood the air mines, which destroyed everything within a radius of a thousand meters.

His wife was crouching before an open fire in the garden trying to boil some water. Next to her sat a cat that had joined them; it had a deep flesh wound on its chest, and its paws were burned. It is worthwhile to speak of the city's cats. They could not be lured from the ruins of their former homes. They slunk about among charred or still smoldering beams, screaming with hunger. When people brought them something out of pity, they would attack the food, screeching, prepared for a fight. But they wouldn't let you pick them up, you had to use force or a ruse. Most of them died despite all the care they were given, either of homesickness or the consuming aftereffects of terror.

The little garden, once hidden and remote in the middle of the city and between tall buildings, was rimed with gray dust. We walked through to the back. My friend spoke incessantly. Here, he said, lay thirty-seven bodies that had burned to death in the cellar. "And look, there's a bloody boot." It was a bombproof cellar, but the doors had jammed. And because the coal bin next to it had caught fire, they had all been roasted alive. They had all fled from the hot walls to the middle of the cellar. There they were found pressed together, bloated from the heat. — "And come up here!" He helped me to climb a hill that had formed there. From the desert that lay beneath us, only the portal of the Konventgarten still stood out. We had heard the Brandenburg Concertos there in April. And a blind woman had sung, "Die schwere Leidenszeit beginnt nun abermals." (The time of suffering now begins once more.) Simple and self-assured, she stood leaning against the harpsichord, and her dead eyes gazed past the vain things for which we were then already trembling; perhaps they were gazing at where we were now. And all that surrounded us now was a sea of stone.

But the poplar tree in the garden had withstood it all like a Damascene blade. Several parakeets had taken shelter among its leaves after fleeing their broken cages. Not only this tree but all of them! With touching haste—in just a few days—they put forth new buds to replace the singed leaves and made a spring for themselves so that they could breathe.

And the three English grandfather clocks in the house had survived as well. When the walls began to quake, they had tottered upright into the room. Why get confused, brothers! Let's keep telling the time, despite all the noise out there. And one of them sounded its little chorale with tender, childlike urgency across the abyss. —

At the university, Misi and I had identity papers made for us. Then we left our heavy luggage with the doorman and headed toward where our home should have been. But it was a detour. Maybe someone will think it is hard to stand in a place where you had lived for many years and where now there is nothing. And that you would then feel crushed by the weight of the

THE END

things that you once called your own. And that then you would sigh or weep. But there is nothing heavy about it, it's just incomprehensible. It is so incomprehensible that it cannot be weighed at all. And how dreadfully heavy that weight is—so heavy that one dares not breathe and moves through the world only with great caution—is almost impossible to put into words.

We stood there three or four times. On the first day, the radiator of the dining room still hung there, way on top. Then that part of the wall collapsed, too, and a few days later the rest was dynamited. Just a small, much too small, heap of stones remained. We kept saying: But that's just not possible. Where is the heavy old table with the lindenwood top? And the chest? There should be a lot more lying there. Also, I could not refrain from peering up sharply to see if the little Madonna had not by chance been left hanging above. But nothing was left, not a single trinket of all the things that we loved and that belonged with us. If there had been such a little something, how we would have caressed it; it would have been imbued with the essence of all the other things. And when we walked on, we left a vacuum behind. And the apartment? Our belongings? It's just not possible. And suddenly it is all there again. You are visiting someone, they have a bookcase. Oh yes! We had so many books. Or they'll put on a record. Do you know this concerto? Yes, that's Handel, we have it ourselves, all we have to do is take it out of the closet. But you know, the Hallelujah Chorus, we play it only on Christmas Eve after setting up the crèche.

It's a family tradition. First the Hallelujah Chorus and then, after the presents, Palestrina. The crown of candles is burning, the other candlesticks too. Which do you think is more beautiful—the big altar light or the little one made of tin? Or the Louis XVI chandelier that always reminded us of grand operas? But you've completely forgotten the white faïence chandelier. Oh, the faïences! They had survived many hundreds of years. They came from Rouen, from Delft, from southern Germany. How many wars there were, and they didn't break. And now?

Or there is just a button that needs to be sewn. Or a roll of yarn is needed. It's all in the game table, next to the récamière. It needs upholstering, by the way, we'll have to take care of that after the war. I'm sure we'll find some old fabric that suits it.

We had that too, we had, had. Not to boast of it, no, but it urges us to speak, it wants to be described, it doesn't want to die. It is not buried beneath the ruins.

But these are just things! Imagine if you had lost your children or your wife. Yes, that is true, we say—but it doesn't change anything. Was our way of living with things wrong, or just different? Who can say? Actually we never owned them. There are vapid books where one finds, again and again, the stupid notion that women want to be possessed and that then they are happy. All the things that surrounded us were only our guests. We respected their separate life, which was older than ours. Sometimes we had a bad conscience because we couldn't offer them what they were used to. A palace or festive rooms. Didn't

THE END

the missals belong in a church? Yes, we will see to it that you return there after we die. But for now—it's so unsafe outside— stay with us and make yourselves at home. We grant you every freedom, we feel responsible for you; we will mute our voices and try to adapt to you.

Or were we their guests? And they gave us indulgent consideration, overlooking our cruder habits, politely avoiding letting us feel the difference of rank between us?

Would it really have been better for them if we had stifled their personality by the power of our urge for possession, thus robbing them of the danger of having a life of their own? No, just—it would be easier for us now. For lost property can be replaced; but—a guest, a friend? Woe to him who would try. We could buy a mirror. Perhaps a connoisseur would say: This mirror is worth more than all the mirrors you used to own. And it would still be no more than a bought replacement. How could it make us forget you whom we love? We granted you every freedom, including the freedom to leave us whenever you wanted. And you left. But we are still here. Don't forget us.

Or was it wrong to live like that after all? Did we misuse things in order to hide behind them from the harshness of reality? But they, defending us, were destroyed, and we now stand naked and without any illusory refuge. This question too must be asked. One must confess or forget, there is no third option.

To forget! A few of those who remained lay on the naked ground of the world. They lay around a fire, men and women.

They were dressed in rags, but they knew nothing else. It was night. There were still stars, the same ones as always. Then someone began to talk in his sleep. No one could understand what he was saying. But they all became uneasy. They got up, they left the fire, they listened anxiously into the cold darkness. They prodded the dreamer with their feet. Then he woke up. "I was dreaming. I must confess what I have dreamt. I was with what lies behind us." He sang a song. The fire turned pale. The women began to weep. "I confess: we were human!" Then the men spoke to one another: "We would freeze to death if what he dreamed were true. Let us kill him!" And they killed him. Then the fire warmed them again, and all were content. —

There was another heavy "could have" in store for us. The first to burden us with it was the old half-lame bread man who was limping ahead of us as we came around the corner onto our street. "My wife still has a suitcase for you," he said. Excited, we ran to the bread store across from our house. The suitcase had stood on the ground floor of a neighbor who had saved it. There was some laundry in it; we were very happy about that. We also worked our way into the cellar of another house not far from ours that had also burnt down. The heat in that cellar was unimaginable, you couldn't stay in it for more than a few minutes. I broke a door open; I was afraid the whole cellar could collapse. There should have been another suitcase of ours there, but it had already been stolen.

THE END

The old bread woman gave us sterilized water to drink, and then she told us: Your house could have been saved. People didn't pay enough attention. At first there was just a small fire in your apartment. Other people confirmed this. Others in turn said: No, there was too much fire right away; in the staircase, too. Still, it seems that conditions during the night of the fire weren't what they should have been. Especially the men who were present did not show enough determination and were only concerned with saving their own possessions. They didn't even open the door of our apartment. — In any case, this much is certain: the fire that destroyed the building came from our apartment. It started during the first minutes of the first night raid.

This "could have" was made harder to bear by the fact that the two buildings next to ours were left standing. Across the way, on the other side of the street, stood another four buildings. But otherwise everything was demolished on all sides. Now it would have been the right thing to ask: How come those few houses were spared? But instead we asked: Why did our house have to be hit? Had we been there, we could have saved it. We always knew no one else would care. — A whole army of "could haves" pursued us after that. At least we could have saved the furs and the shoes and some of our linen. Maybe this or that keepsake. Why didn't we think of sending away some of our things like everyone else? We didn't even put the silverware or the jewelry into a safe. It would have been easy, but you never wanted to. But at least the journals ....

The journals? Yes, now I realize they no longer exist. I kept a journal for twenty-five years. "Journal" is actually not the right word, for there were hardly any events recorded in it, only the thoughts that were prompted by events. No, not thoughts, either, but rather my way of arriving at them. Yes, what I was recording was the process of thinking. I would never have looked through these notebooks again, by the way; they disgusted me. Why did I keep writing in them at all, intermittently but still for twenty-five years? Indeed, why am I writing this? — No, even though it is incomprehensible that they are gone, these twenty-five years, this trace, this path, how can one be concerned with saving this sort of record? Surely that would be indecent. If anything ought to be left to its fate, it is things like this.

We found a stronger "could have" to pit against that one. We told ourselves: We could have been hit, we probably would have; or maybe just one of us. Because we would have been upstairs in the apartment, as always. —But didn't you often tell me, when I got worried, that we wouldn't get hit?

Yes, and in fact we didn't.

For three years I said: I won't get hit. And the one standing next to me won't get hit either. Let the buildings fall right and left; there is nothing to fear. — I didn't say it often; I especially did not say it out loud. For as soon as it is spoken, it becomes false and worthless; you can only know it. And there was only one time—it was night, and outside they were shooting again—

THE END

when I knew why I would not be hit, and I told you, too: Because fate does not want to let me off so lightly.

The buildings right and left are still standing, but ours is gone. What was it, then, that impelled us to leave so shortly before it happened, like animals suddenly forced to abandon their old burrows? They don't know why, and a little later an earthquake erupts.

We don't want to question it, we are willing to bear the heavier burden. Is this it already? Who knows. At the moment when we turn away from the ruins of our former home, there begins a path that leads beyond and away from the end.

It started with our getting swept up by the flood of people returning to Hamburg, which set in with elemental force. There was nothing drawing them back, no one was calling them. On the contrary, the walls are still covered with official notices warning against unauthorized returns, even threatening punishments. But the authorities were powerless against this urge, and in order to save face, they issued a new edict: Those who do not return will be prosecuted.

But what was it that drove people back to the city? They all said: Better to live in a cellar hole under the ruins than lead a tolerated existence somewhere else. But that's just a negative explanation. Or did they mean that here, where their house used to stand, they had rights and could make demands and would not have to beg? Is it what was left to us of the idea of "home"? Or is it just a law of inertia—the drops that were hurled in all directions by the city's collapse now flooding back into the crater?

And there began the tortuous search for a makeshift shelter. The appeals to the authorities. The anxious rush to acquire an earthenware plate. And this touching, childlike joy in the faces of people striding homeward with a package under their arm, as if for once they had gotten the better of fate. And those who saw it asked, full of envy and curiosity: Where can you buy that? And yet it was just a thing, so undignified in its shape and material that people would once have been ashamed of it.

But that already doesn't belong here.

Is it the heaviness? People are trying to behave as if life were going on as before. Things have gotten a little tighter, it's gotten harder to make ends meet, but look, we're practicing our profession again, crossing the street as if nothing had happened, the women are dressing up. But....

They know it's just an appearance. They don't believe in it. The stage sets are missing, the illusion of reality. In front of a burnt out house I saw an allegory of this. Lying on top of the rubble in the front yard was the harplike frame of a grand piano. Through the charred debris and the broken springs, a rose had grown and was blooming. It was like a picture on an old cup. In the past, people would not have hesitated to write beneath it, "To bloom and to perish."

Yes, when evening falls, everyone says: We want to own just a few things so that nothing will hold us back and we can run

THE END

away more easily. They say it as if it were a matter of course that from time to time one has to run away from *something*....It's unavoidable. It can't be explained, but you have to make allowances for it.

Have people made themselves lighter so as to make the heaviness more bearable? Sometimes someone will say: This is just the beginning. Someday we'll look back on this with nostalgia. There will be famines, epidemics, and whatnot. Only a quarter of us will survive. Nothing can be done about it. You have to be lucky. — All this is quite possible. In the meantime, other cities have been laid waste, some are burning at this moment, and those that have been spared so far are awaiting their hour with dread. Already Hamburg's calamity no longer counts.

Does it no longer count because the ones to be pitied are not we who already have it behind us, but those who still stand at the edge of the abyss, doubting that they can surmount it, because they are still thinking the way one had to think on the other side, squeezed in between yesterday and tomorrow, without a second of presence? For what we have gained and what has changed is this: We have become present. We have slipped away from the precincts of time. Time still keeps watch over us, she orders us to work and calls us to lunch, and we obey. Sometimes we fail to heed her call, because we were enriched by an object we had not previously recognized, and then she scolds us: How dreamy you all are. But the punishment doesn't affect our inmost nature. Dear, poor Time, why are you so upset? We will gladly do whatever you want if it makes you happy and keeps you from getting angry. — You're not to keep going to that stranger, says Time, I'm going to lock you up. — Oh, Mother, why not? — He'll spoil you, and you won't amount to anything in life. — Mother, you don't know him. He knows such beautiful games. He lives over there, where there are no more houses. Every afternoon he comes through the old archway. He is our friend. We always ask him to take us to where he lives. But he doesn't want to, not yet; he says: Just wait a while, children. Wouldn't you like to meet him too, Mother? — No! And you're staying here now. He's not proper company for you.

Our mother has many more things to do; she washes, she cooks, and in between she has to go to the cellar to fetch coal. When she comes back up, the children have left. She goes to the window and hears them singing:

Maikäfer, flieg,
Mein Vater ist im Krieg,
Mein Mutter ist in Pommerland,
Pommerland ist abgebrannt.

[Ladybug, fly,
My father's in the war,
My mother is in Pomerania,
Pomerania's all burnt down.]

THE END

We have run back out on the street and are playing with Death. Now Time sits down sadly in a corner and feels useless. —

The hardest part is already behind us; the harder doesn't count in comparison. It's not so bad. I heard this said by a man who did not know that he was saying it. He was one of the countless multitude, anyone else could have said it. He told me about his night and how it tried to destroy him. He did it in the manner we all have when we talk about it. Four notes are enough. How sad that sounds, says the mind. But it isn't sad, it's just how it is. The truly sad thing is the mind, because it thinks it has wings, but it keeps falling back to earth.

And the one who told me his story did not know that with his imageless language he was creating an image such as no poet can create. He said:

Then a man came into the cellar and told us, you've got to come out now, the whole house is burning, it's going to collapse any minute. Most of us didn't want to, they thought they'd be safe where they were. But they all died. Some of us listened to him. But it took a lot to do that. We had to go out through a hole, and in front of the hole the flames were beating back and forth. It's not so bad, he said, look, I came in to get you, don't you see? So I wrapped a wet blanket around my head and crawled out. Then we were through it. Some people keeled over in the street then. We couldn't take care of them.

NOVEMBER 1943

Erich Andres (1905–1992) has been called "the man with the ladder" because he would often carry one on his treks through Hamburg, looking for the best angle for shots that would tell stories. By the late 1920s he was well known for clever human interest pictures of Hamburg and its people. He shot in the Balkans, at the Berlin Olympics, and during the civil war in Spain. In 1939 he was drafted to serve in a propaganda company for the Luftwaffe and photographed for the military through the end of the war. After 1945 Andres concentrated on scenes of daily life for the popular press.

On home leave in July of 1943, he was able to take unauthorized pictures immediately after Operation Gomorrah but hid the negatives until after the war. Andres is an especially narrative photographer and often uses irony. One famous image is of boys looking at photos of unattainable movie stars through the glass of a shop window. Here, though, the antitheses are grim: the coal bucket and carbonized corpses, the man on the bench in front of a ruined streetscape, the mute bell, the stopped clock on the tower.

SCOTT DENHAM

THE END

ERICH ANDRES

PHOTOGRAPHS

COLOPHON

The design and typography of this book are by William Drenttel and Don Whelan of Winterhouse Studio, in Falls Village, Connecticut. The text is composed in Lexicon, a typeface designed in 1992 by Bram de Does for The Enschedé Font Foundry in Haarlem, The Netherlands. The headings are set in Gotham, designed by Tobias Frere-Jones with Jesse Ragan in 2002 for The Hoefler Type Foundry.